Every... g

BY

Ian M. Small

IDEAS UNLIMITED (PUBLISHING)

Published by:
Ideas Unlimited (Publishing)
P.O. Box 125, Portsmouth
Hampshire PO1 4PP

ISBN: 1 871964 12 1

Limericks by Michael Walsh and Liz Garrad

Cartoons by Willy Sanker

Printed & Bound in Hong Kong

TO THE SMALLEST AND LOVELIEST GUY I KNOW

REMEMBER *'VERY LITTLE'* CAN COME BETWEEN US
IF YOU PLAY YOUR CARDS RIGHT!

LOVE

....

XXX

Acknowledgements

I would like to thank Ian Small for his invaluable insight into the psychology of dealing with this problem, in such a way that it will help to bring many out of the closet.

Michael Walsh, for his excellent limericks which through an extraordinary wit gives a happy note to a sad situation.

Liz Garrad for her outstanding limericks which give a refreshing view of the problem from a woman's point of view.

Willy Sanker for his amusing cartoons which give another dimension to a sad situation.

Finally to Dick Small for his time and sincere response to our exclusive interview, which I hope will go towards changing public opinion and better standards for his future generations.

Introduction

"NO ONE IS PERFECT"

This is a well known fact which has been acknowledged since time began. O.K. ... So some may be more imperfect than others, the fact remains that we all have something we would change about ourselves, given the choice.

Unfortunately, that choice is very rarely given, and so we have to learn to live with our little imperfections. Fortunately, in most cases we do manage to live quite contented with our problems.

There is however, just one little imperfection that we just can't handle, and that is having a small willy. Men can live quite happily having just one arm, and even paralysed, be short-sighted with bad breath, receding hair-line and covered with acne. To them that's just life. But you mention that they may have a small willy, and they will go wild, depression will set in, and they may even consider suicide.

WHY? ... Why is this such an intolerable problem for most men? Well I'll tell you ... I DON'T KNOW!!
All I know is that it is, and here all we can offer is a kind of self-help book for sufferers to deal with their problem. It is based on such self-help books as "How to deal with the grief of losing a loved one", except in our case it is "How to deal with the grief of not finding 'the loved one'."

Contents

THE PROBLEM
Don't be like Mark
Your worst nightmare
Bragging can backfire
Insensitive ego shatterers

THE SOLUTION
Boosting your ego
Small Dicks Anonymous
Positive Thinking
The amateur bullshitter
The Professional bullshitter
Don't push your luck
The case for the defence
It's not my problem
Get your own back
Silicone implants
Do not despair

THINGS YOU CANNOT DO
Keep away from nude beaches
Worry about the size of your nose
Stay in the closet

The Contents

Tattoos are not for you
Modesty pays in a foreign land
The painful search
Don't let the bastards give you away

THE EXCLUSIVE INTERVIEW

GLIMMER OF HOPE
Is size really important
Cute little dicks beauty contest
Not all women go for size
Being big is not always fun
What do women prefer

IS THERE ANYTHING WORSE
SHOW CONFIDENCE
YOU ARE NOT ALONE
YOU KNOW YOU HAVE A PROBLEM IF ...

SUGGESTED DIET & EXERCISE

KEEP A CHART
A FRIEND IN NEED
HOW TO USE YOUR FREE GIFT

Don't Be Like Mark

Whenever the subject of small willies is mentioned, I always remember my friend Mark. He was very unfortunate in that, not only did he have a small willy, but to his horror, a few people knew about it. Everyone teased him, and he was forever trying to stop the rumour from spreading, but to no avail.

One night whilst enjoying a drink with a girl on their first date, he was horrified to hear the stand up comedian start cracking jokes about small willies. It kept on getting worse. The comedian after mentioning Mark's name and pointing him out, even made others in the club look at him and say "Ahhhh".
This happened a couple of times, and Mark was so enraged that he set off for revenge. He consulted the best comedy writers in the country, had meetings with the best comedians on TV, and at great expense worked out a line, which he could use next time the comedian made fun of his small willy.
So one night whilst having a drink, he awaited the jokes and ridicule to start, and as soon as they did, he got up, looked straight at the comedian and with a loud voice said:

"Why don't you just shut up, OK?"

Needless to say, that didn't really do the trick, but happily Mark has stopped going to that club.

You need not be as helpless as Mark, and hopefully by the end of this book, you will be a lot more prepared for those difficult situations.

Your Worst Nightmare

The little problem which you were not sure you had, becomes very apparent during a supposedly pleasurable encounter with the opposite sex. It will be an innocent remark, but to you it will be the realisation of a painful fact.

She lay supine upon her back,
Her dress was pulled up high;
Her thighs apart for him to start,
He heard her moan and sigh.

"Oh, put it in, don't tease me so –
You really are a one!
I've closed my eyes – is it a size ...
... Are all your flies undone?"

He crouched behind the kneeling maid,
And thrust it in and out –
Was just about to orgasm ...
When she began to shout.

"Oh put it in, don't tease me so –
You really are a one!
I've closed my eyes – is it a size ...
... Are all your flies undone?"

Your Worst Nightmare

Bragging Can Backfire

Compensating for an undersized dick, by excessive bragging is quite common. Just be warned that it could back-fire on you, during that painful moment when you have to reveal all.

"Now close the door – before you score;
I want to see your willy.
I never lay for men who say,
Their size is something silly.
Like near a foot, ten inch or more,
They're always telling lies;
You men make all the promises,
Before you split your flies."

He flashed his prong, it wasn't long ...
Perhaps three inches-no-more;
And then she started laughing,
And she laughed till she was sore.
"You'll hardly need a lubricant,
Oh, really have a care.
To prise it in, you'll need a pin,
To get it past the hair.

It may be a good idea to tell a joke just at the moment when you are about to take your shorts off. That way she may well be laughing at your joke.

Bragging Can Backfire

I'd heard his technique was fantastic,
That to him sex was truly a craft,
Then he took his shorts off
and I spluttered and coughed,
collapsed on the floor and just laughed.

Insensitive Ego Shatterers

Women can be very cruel when it comes to your little predicament. In most cases you can dismiss those hurtful comments, because they don't really know you as a person. But when the cruelty comes from those closest to you, it's intolerable and down right embarrassing, particularly if you have company at the time.

"Another puzzle you might solve,"
The compere sang out loud;
We had our pencils ready while,
he gazed across the crowd.

"Two inches long, it's white as well ...
Its tip is brightest red?"
What do you think that it could be,
"A match I guess" said Fred.

"A birthday candle, short and thin?"
I answered with a shrug –
"Without the head that's coloured red;
Perhaps a garden slug?"

"I'm not so sure," said Cathy Moore,
Fred's wife, she was no fool.
"I think he's seen that dick of yours –
It sound just like your tool."

Boosting Your Ego

"Take it out, you're hurting me!"
The pretty hooker cried.
"It's much too big, don't move it so,"
The street girl cooed and sighed.

"Oh, please, I can't take another inch,"
I've never known ... It's ... ohhhh!"
You mustn't do that; it's so big –
You musn't hurt me so."

When Sam was spent, his penis bent,
He buttoned up his flies.
He gave a Fiver for the screw –
And twenty for the lies.

Protecting your ego has got to be your main task. Once that is shattered, then your problem becomes very apparent. It will be like having it tattooed on your forehead, "I HAVE A SMALL WILLY." So it is worthwhile to opt for the occasional ego booster, perhaps not as far fetched as the example above.

Other ego boosters are discussed later on in this book.

Join the SDA (Small Dicks Anonymous)

A recent survey carried out proved that more than 22% of the population suffer from 'The Tiny Problem'. Unfortunatley most of these people are still going through the denial phase, which means they still prefer to keep the problem well buttoned-up.

Some of you however, having passed that phase and into the acceptance phase, are more likely to come up with a solution for the rebuilding of that most-important self-confidence.

Being with others with the same problem and sharing experiences is your first task. Find out if there is an SDA club in your town and, if not, start one by inviting all of those people you suspect of sharing the problem. By joining forces, you may even be able to change public opinion on small dicks. But for starters a few basic rights will suffice.

No groups or self-help bodies
for us guys with dongs so small;
No organised committees, no grants – just nowt at all.
There's alcoholics plenty and of gamblers there's afew
But if you have a little dick; what can we victims do?

Organise and militate, demand our rights! Okay!
Let's lobby, march, petition – and we'll form the SDA
Small Dicks Anon and thereupon, let's organise and fight
For dildos on prescription and transplants another right.

S.D.A. (Small Dicks Anonymous)

The Power of Positive Thinking

You must not underestimate the power of Positive Thinking. It has helped many with more serious problems and there is no reason why it should not help you.

I myself had a problem and was advised to try Positive Thinking. I reluctantly tried it, but didn't think it would work and sure enough it didn't.

He pulled the chick and then he hoped,
His dick would soon respond.
He had a cosy little place –
where he could screw the blonde.

But on the bed, it should be said,
His dick just wouldn't rise;
He dreamed he was a melon large,
That it could share its size.

He thought about bananas,
But the lunchbox did the trick –
The tender meat, that awesome treat;
It made him 'super dick'.

The Power of Positive Thinking

The Amateur Bullshitter

The bullshitting part of being small; the padding, the lying and pretending that you are bigger than you really are, is truly an

artform. You may begin with the very basics, but through time you will discover hidden talents you never knew you had.

Don't Push Your Luck

As you probably know, having a small dick need not necessarily affect the way you pull the girls. You can learn to impress women with lies, pretence and even reverse psychology. You can make out that you suffer from the problem of being too big for most women.

These lies will normally do the trick and you will succeed in chatting up the girl of your dreams. But getting greedy and expecting to pull it off all the way through sex, may constitute you being a little optimistic!

However good you may be, women always have a way of finding out (usually once sex starts) that you are not what you made out to be.

This is usually a very big blow and an unbearable disappointment to women. To demonstrate this, let me explain through a verse which might strike a cord with one or two of you ...

You never took the mickey
When I held you to my chest
I caressed your perfect body,
Tenderly I pressed
I wanted you to marry me, I would have told you but,
You started to frown, you lost air and went down,
and collapsed in a heap on my foot!

Or You Will Come Unstuck

The Case for the Defence

Surveys show that women feel very comfortable with guys who have smaller-than-average dicks. This is because they can humiliate the guy to their heart's desire. You must therefore be prepared with a few good defence lines, in which you plead not guilty and pass the buck.

She said "My you've got a small organ"
As she gazed at my willy with awe.
I replied "That is true ...
But until I met you ...
I'd not played a cathedral before."

Or your defence lines can be structured in such a way as to question the whole idea of SIZE. Something small to some people, may be HUGE to others given the right situation. Arguing this will probably bore her into submission, before you need to prove your point. This may be illustrated in the following verse ...

She watched me come out of the shower,
She asked "Is it cold?" with a grin,
I replied "Well my dear, you'd not like it I fear ...
If a wart grew this big on your chin."

Another type of defence line is of course going for that sympathy vote, as illustrated on the opposite page. This will make them feel so small, that they wish they were as big as your willy.

The Sympathy Vote Defence Line

It's Not My Problem

Denial, anger, acceptance, deceit and passing-the-buck are usually the phases guys with small dicks go through. Without a doubt, the only enjoyable one is the passing-the-buck phase.

Size isn't everything
that simply isn't true,
Can you ever recall the time
when a woman said to you,
"You are really great between the sheets"
Delivered with a snigger
"You are really great, I promise you,
But I wish your dick was bigger"
They are never satisfied
with the dimensions of your member,
they always wish it extra large
you know, just to remember.
But has the thought occurred to them,
A thought not too uncanny
That the fault may actually lie with them
And that they need a tighter fanny!

I Don't have a Problem

Get Your Own Back

You must always be a step ahead of some women. Let them know that they too suffer from a size problem.

My wife was in the bath one night,
I paused to ask of she;
"If you could change your figure, Dear,
What would you like to see?"

"I'm glad you asked me that" she said
"I'll get it off my chest,
What I could change about myself?
I'd like much bigger breasts."

"They never bounce or wobble;
Just like I want them to;
A thirty eight or forty!
That's what I'd like for you."

"Might I suggest some Andrex,
That tissue for the loo
And rub it up between your tits
And see what that will do."

"You think Andrex could really work?
That it would make them bigger?"
"I'm sure of it" I said to her,
... She didn't see me snigger.

"Just rub it once between your tits:
You'll be a comely lass
They'll soon be Dolly Parton big –
It worked upon your ass."

ANDREX
TOILET TISSUE

Can Medical Science Help?

Why so many men worry about the size of their dicks is beyond me. With medical science, today you can change, add or take away any part of your body you desire. Silicone Implantation has been practised on women's breasts for years now and it's just a matter of time before it becomes common for men. It is at present in its experimental stage, but you being as desperate as you are, may wish to take the risk and help science.

The silicone op' was a failure;
His dick was too low on his thigh;
So when Sam went out to his dancing,
He often heard young maidens cry.

"Oh, heavens above, have a mercy,
Your dick is right down to your knee.
If such is its length when we're dancing,
I can't bed you now you'll agree."

So Sam never did get his pleasure,
It had quite the other effect.
A dick reaching half down your trousers,
Is a turn-off, a penile defect.

Treat Yourself to a Silicone Job

Do Not Despair, I See A Light

Life is just not fair; there are those who have so much that they waste, whilst there are others who live in poverty.
You may consider certain measures to overcome your little problem as a little far-fetched. But the fact of the matter is that most guys are at their wits end with this problem, and are prepared to try anything. Some of these measures, however far-fetched, do turn out to do the trick.

The circumcision clinic was the only place to be;
For Bert who has a tiny dick and clearly wants to see
Between his thighs, a mighty rise, a penis long and thick;
For girls will sigh, will claim to die to see a turbo prick.

He hung about the clinic, if you sort of get my drift;
And glanced about, approached the bin, its lid began to lift.
Discarded bits of penises; I guess it should be known;
That some were thick, and others long;
much bigger than his own;

Of transplants there were many and old Bert he had a choice;
Of super dicks, so many pricks – the girls would all rejoice,
At last he found a whopper and he soon had it attached,
It even came with pubic hairs,
and splendid balls to match.

Do Not Despair

Keep Away From Beaches

Beaches and swimming pools are really not the place to be, unless of course you have other plans to outsmart the onlookers.

Jet-lagged, unpacked but mustard-keen
to pose where breakers roar;
Ben picked a pair of swimming trunks
to use down by the shore.
In Dayglo red and yellow, oh, those briefs were really loud;
He'd soon be on that sun-kissed beach.
He'd stand out in the crowd.

And then he had an after-thought, inspired and rather fun;
He skinned a huge banana and as soon as it was done,
He took the skin and tied it round his rather tiny prick;
Which then appeared much larger
and perhaps three times as thick.

"Oh boy! Won't this impress them!" The mirror seemed to say.
Quite clearly he was donkey-rigged and something of a lay;
A mighty bulge no one could match,
around him they would flock;
To see the bulge that hinted at a truly mighty cock.

He reached the beach, a swagger told of arrogance and pride;
Heads were turned, and envy burned
and eyes were opened wide.
But then poor Ben was shattered
and his face turned white as bleach;
He'd chanced upon – officially – the only nudist beach!

Disaster On The Beach

Worry About the Size of Your Nose

Some smart bastards in the scientific field have come up with theories which state that the size of a person's willy is proportional to the size of his nose. As you will appreciate this marks a major set-back for those of us who have mastered the art of pretending we have a bigger willy than we actually do. It is now like wearing your dick on your face, for the whole world to see and ridicule to their hearts content.

But we have to be strong. We will not be beaten, even if it means taking steps to change the size of our nose, just to confuse those bastards.
So the following are ways in which you can overcome this by enlarging the size of your nose:

a) Obviously the easiest is to apply a few big punches on your nose. If you find it difficult, you can always ask a friend or even enemy, who would be only too happy to oblige.

b) Sticking your nose in the doorway, and slamming the door shut, is another popular method.

c) Finally, if you cannot tolerate pain, you can always try the 'Godfather' method of padding your nose wtih cotton wool, tissues etc. If they managed to fool millions in the Godfather movie by padding the cheeks, there is no reason why you cannot successfully fool people by padding your nose.

Don't Let Your Nose Give You Away

Stay in the Closet

Having a small dick kind of restricts you from indulging in certain pastimes. Nothing against you ... It's just like a convicted criminal serving life can't indulge in politics and the opportunity of leading the country.

You may well be ready to come out of the closet, but the world may not; and their cruel response could damage that valuable self-confidence you worked so hard to build. So stay in the closet and keep away from those enjoyable public exhibitions.

Old Dick the renowned flasher
was inclined to shock and scare,
He'd open up his dirty mac –
the girls would gasp and stare,
One day he saw two hookers
though he thought them undefined;
He flashed old Dick the dirty prick;
he thought he'd drive them wild.

One laughed, oh, how she chortled
till the tears came in her eyes,
Humiliating Dick the Flash,
whose prick just wouldn't rise,
"I've seen a bigger worm," she cried,
"In apples old and rotten,
Close your coat, you silly goat!
Once seen, it's best forgotten."

No Public Exhibitions

Tattoos Are Not For You

Dear Marge,
I went to this tatooist
To have my name put on my knob.
She looked at my dong
And said "Your name's too long."
Have you any suggestions,?
Love, Rob!

Agony Aunts will not be able to help you. You must have to try and rise above the ridicule. Who cares how many words you can have stet on your dick?

In the toilets last year in Jamaica
I stood there and stared at the floor
While a native all cool
Uncoiled his tool
And stood three feet away at the door
Tatooed on the length of his member
Were the words 'Jamaica and Die'
I thought well that's fine
And looked down at mine
It looked back at me and said 'Hi'!

Tattoos Are Not For You

Modesty Pays in a Foreign Land

However well-travelled you are, it is worth remembering that you are in unfamiliar surroundings and the most important lesson is to keep your mouth shut.

T'was Wendy this and Wendy that,
he really loved that chick;
So much he even had her name tattooed upon his dick.
But when it was just normal size, an inch perhaps, no more;
The 'W' and 'Y' alone was all his girlfriend saw.

He took her to Jamaica and went 'native' on the beach,
Steel bands an' that, he looked a twat –
but she was quite a peach.
He liked the local colour and he joined the fun with zest;
And in the public showers Wendy's man was quite impressed.

So it was true, there were a few,
black swingers of some note;
Of no mean size, he envied them – it really got his goat.
One caught his eye and he could see a tattoo like his own,
A 'W' and yes, a 'Y' were both quite clearly shown.

Intrigued he asked the bather if his girl was 'Wendy' too.
The guy then smiled and shook his head,
and played until it grew;
Then Wendy's man could better scan and saw the tattoo say;
'Welcome to Jamaica, and do enjoy your staY'.

Excuse Me, But ...

The Painful Search

As if the pain of having a small dick is not enough, some men are even accused of not having a dick at all. This invariably results in long hard searches with tweezers, long finger-nails and most dangerous of all magnifying glasses.

Why can't women just take our word that it's there somewhere, instead of subjecting us to those painful searches.

For she who dares, his pubic hairs.
If she would seek to find,
Amidst the bush his manhood lay –
When she would wish to grind.

But first she had to find the dick;
She used her spying glass.
His boxer shorts she then pulled out
And wriggled with her ass.

Her practiced eye would seek it out,
His flaccid little worm –
Embarrassed, Dan would blush with shame,
He'd look askance and squirm.

The sun was past her shoulders,
And its rays shone through the glass,
And laser-beamed his dick to zilch.
– He now masturbates his lass.

Missing In Action

Don't Let the Bastards Give You Away

The worst thing that could happen is for a rumour to start that you have a small dick. Before you know it everyone knows, so you must therefore avoid giving cause for any such rumours to start. If you start missing out on routine activities such as taking a shower with the lads after the game, they will suspect that you have something to hide. So take part, but be prepared. There is nothing wrong with wanting your dick to be extra clean, and therefore using a little more foam than others. What you must remember, however, is that you never rinse the soap. After all, it's the soap that kills the germs, so why rinse it off?

When you are with the lads, you must keep the subject well away from dicks. Most popular conversation is cracking jokes about women.

They sat and watched the world go by
And Harry paused to say,
"My wife and I, we never talk,
When making love each day."

"Do you old friend, talk to your wife,
When making love and randy?"

"Only if, beside the bed,
There is a phone that's handy!"

Use Extra Foam in Public

THE REPORTER: There has been a lot of media coverage on the subject of size. There is a lot of dissatisfaction about ... Women feel cheated for being short-changed, and men are going through personality transformations, becoming liars and cheats just to prove they are not really small. A lot of people have been pointing the finger at you. What do you have to say for yourself?

DICK: People are always very quick to point the finger at us; but do they ever stop to think how we feel; what life is like for us? Size is the least of my problems. It is not easy being a dick. I have a head I cannot think with, an eye I cannot see through, I have to hang around with two nuts all day, my closest neighbour is an asshole, and my best friend is a pussy. Now because of AIDS I have to wear this rubber coat and throw up on my self.
Being small is my way of protesting for better standards of living, it's my way of attracting attention. Call me a terrorist, if you wish, at least I have the guys by the balls.

The Exclusive Interview

Is Size Really Important?

Most guys assume that all women consider size important. That simply isn't true. I am sure there are many guys with small dicks who are fantastic lovers; just as there must be many mass-murderers who value life.

The bird was cute; he'd screw tonight,
sure as his name was Mick.
But would the night be blemished
when she saw his tiny dick?
A shameful situation which would now be met head on,
He asked her, "Would you far prefer to have a little one?"

"Oh no! I really do prefer to have a little one.
Who needs it large or oversize when all is said and done?"
Relief was on Mick's features that at last he'd found a bird;
Who wouldn't mock his tiny cock
that made him look absurd.

But sadly there's an ending
that poor Mick could not foresee,
"I'll diet, that is what I'll do, for it is plain to see;
My bum's too fat – now fancy that! You have a little dick.
You don't intend to screw with that –
is this some kind of trick?"

Is Size Really Important?

'Cute Little Dicks' Beauty Contest

The idea of a beauty contest for the smallest dick is nothing new. Since its debut a few years ago in a small town in South Korea, these contests are really catching on. It is only a matter of time before it becomes an international contest or even part of the Olympics. So don't despair, you may well be sitting on a gold mine, if you pardon the expression.

Just as Buxom women were admired in days of old;
With ample breasts and thighs to match,
won hearts of knights so bold,
It came to pass, some said ALAS! but thin girls lit the fire;
The mode was slim, the boyish look
was what we'd all desire.

But fashion, fate and fortune turned
the wheel the small man's way –
For men with little private parts were flavour of the day;
Contests were held unparalleled,
for dicks all shrivelled small –
Two-inch dicks were in demand,
but the bigger not at all.

The dames would be the judges
and with eyeglass and soft touch;
They'd go upon the podium and feel them round the crutch,
Small was judged to win the day –
and still that day may come
Dream on my friend, and keep your dick,
no bigger than my thumb!

SMALL
is BEAUTIFUL
~ CHAMPIONSHIP ~
1
2
3
IT IS THERE HONEST

Not All Women Go For Size

It is simply not true to say that size is everything to all women. To prove this, we conducted a comprehensive survey, and sure enough our findings prove that, without a shadow of a doubt, there are a number of women to whom size is not important.

The survey was all proper and a hundred thousand dames;
– SAVE THREE – agreed, size was indeed
essential to love's game.
"It's got to be a whopper." was the common view upheld,
Eight inches long the perfect prong
and must be self-propelled.

Three girls were asked but disagreed,
one shook her pretty head;
"I far prefer a little one," the nervous virgin said.
"Not for me a big one!" then said the tiny dwarf;
"Wot ist you ask, no understand,"
Said Zi from Dusseldorf.

Not All Women Go For Size

Being Big Is Not All It's Made Out To Be

The guys with small dicks have got it made. Can you imagine the pain you would encounter if you were big out of all proportion?

You can get them long and thin,
You can get them short and thick.
You can get them that lasts for hours
And there's them that's over quick.
You can get them in all colours
From pale pink to jet black too
But I stamped on yours an hour ago
And bugger me it's blue!

O.K., You may say that the pain is worth it, but what good are you to anyone if you pass out from the pain? O.K.? You may be right again, silly question.

I know I am not built like a donkey
I'm small and of that there's no doubt.
If I had half a yard, I might fail to get hard
And then when I did I'd pass out!

Lastly, here's one advantage of being small you can't argue with. You can sit on the beach, watch sexy women go by, and no one will ever know you are excited.

The Joke Is On You Big Guy

What Do Women Prefer?

Given the choice, which would you rather be:

a) A hunk of a guy with a tiny dick, or
b) An ugly little guy with a large dick.

This is the dilemma facing a lot of women. Should they go for the hunk who seems too perfect to be true, so he must have a worm for a dick, or should they choose the ugly guy whose undesirable looks are probably compensated for by having a large dick. This is in fact the reasoning behind a lot of ugly guys pulling the chicks.

Now what a cruel dilemma
that would make a girl's heart ache;
The ugly guy with quite a bulge? oh, what a choice to make.
For she could also opt instead for 'James Bond' by his side,
Whose front was flat! Her heart or Twat?
But now she must decide.

It was her twat that won the day,
the ugly one was picked;
Handsome hunks were plenty but she wanted to be pricked;
By something rare and wonderful, a donkey-dick at least;
A sight so right; she'd seen the light – it really seemed a feast.

It came to pass, she bared her ass,
his trousers were undone,
He dropped his briefs, was ready for no end of sexy fun ...
But he had pulled a fast one;
he was cute and he was chuffed –
He'd got some big bananas
and his briefs were really stuffed.

Is There Anything Worse?

Sure ... Having a small dick is a problem, but you must always remember that there are always others worse off than you. What you have never had you will not miss; think of those who had size but lost it.

The Madame showed distaste
and the prostitutes made haste,
To refuse the poor dwarf's need and coin;
For the tiny little man, who they each would clearly ban,
Had his head on a level with their groin.

One whore she relented and he paid as she consented
To the room up the stairs they repaired;
She was blonde and a beauty,
who would clearly do her duty
And she smiled and he grinned till she bared.

He quickly followed suit and my God he had a beaut'
And she screamed till they ran through the door
He was standing there undressed
and by God they were impressed,
For his dong it was touching the floor.

Two feet long, what a prong
and it now stood stiff and strong;
"Can I touch it?" the Madame did call;
"Just a touch, not too much ... but I'll never let you suck –
For I once was quite big, six feet tall."

Show Confidence At All Times

The more confident you are about yourself, the more faith people will have in you and the less likely they are to notice your short-fall.

He walked into the chemist's shop,
with confidence and style.
The pretty young assistant though,
Was miserable – no smile.

"I have two dates this weekend so –
I have to dress my cock!
I need to have some condoms, Miss;
What kind are kept in stock?"

She showed him what she had to show –
But angry all the same.
Familiarity turned her off –
She was a snooty dame.

"Two packs of ribbed, I'll have please, Miss!"
She glared, "Please don't Miss me!"
"Suit yourself," The guy replied,
"You'd better make it three."

You Know You Have A Problem If ...

1. You find yourself repeatedly using phrases like:
    a) "All good things come in small packages"
    b) "It's not the quantity, it's the quality"
    c) "There is more to sex than a big dick"
    d) "Size isn't everything"
2. You insist on foreplay with your clothes on.
3. You dislike beaches, swimming pools, public showers and changing rooms.
4. When using a public toilet, you prefer to go into the cubicle.
5. In the bedroom, it's always far too cold to go completely naked; unless of course the light is out.
6. You look at certain fruits and vegetables with envy.
7. You love the humour of using exotic condoms.
8. Your hands always feel cold and you must therefore always keep them in your pocket.
9. You are forever checking your flies, as the consequences of an open fly for you would be disastrous. It would be one sure way to give yourself away:

I knew he was a comic
I knew before he spoke
'Cause his flies were gaping open
To reveal his little joke.

10. Your day to day clothing, and even those chosen for fancy dress parties are a little overdone with the padding or scope for padding.

You Are Not Alone

The small dick syndrome is a problem shared by millions of guys. Most go through life concealing the problem well. This ability to conceal your problem, is a luxury you would not have if you were fat, bald, ugly or covered with acne.

It may be heartening to know that even some of the perfect looking guys also suffer from this problem.

Your muscles are truly outstanding
Your eyes are dark brown and they twinkle.
You're bright, you're no fool,
But you've not got a tool,
Just a couple of prunes and a wrinkle.

So Stand Up and be Counted/Measured

Diet and Exercise Will Help

As any doctor or expert would tell you, diet and exercise can work wonders in shaping up your body. The suggested diet, as set out on the opposite page, is guaranteed to work in enlarging your little problem, if carried out as instructed. Exercise is also very important, and must be taken up at every possible opportunity.

He exercised till he was weary;
And used it to hang up his towel.
When building a kitchen extension,
He used it instead of a trowel.

His theory was right, it was proper;
To use it or lose it he held.
If he was to have a real whopper,
That was turbo and rocket-propelled.

He would exercise relevant muscles,
Would use it whenever he could.
He would screw everything that was moving;
He would bed all the great and the good.

He would diet and try it so often,
To keep in the shape that required;
A guy to be tops in performance –
And screw everything he desired.

So it grew as he knew it should oughta;
So big he could suck it, he joked –
And one day he did so and farted –
And died when he spluttered and choked.

Suggested Diet

DAY OF THE WEEK	THE DIET TO PROMOTE EXTRA GROWTH
MONDAY	
breakfast	Unpeeled bananas
lunch	Salad made of uncut cucumbers and tomatoes
dinner	Fried courgette with new potatoes
TUESDAY	
breakfast	A few slices of toast cut into soldiers
lunch	Wholesome raw aubergines
dinner	Uncut carrots, swallowed whole
WEDNESDAY	
breakfast	Banana milkshake with extra whole bananas
lunch	Cucumber supreme and whole onions
dinner	Corn on the cob
THURSDAY	
breakfast	Banana long-boat without the boat
lunch	Sausages
dinner	Carrot surprise
FRIDAY	
breakfast	Bubble & squeak
lunch	Chilli meat with spiced nuts
dinner	Curried snake
SATURDAY	
breakfast	Banana surprise
lunch	Calves' tongues
dinner	Barbecued turkey necks
SUNDAY	
breakfast	Black pudding
lunch	Frankfurters and brussels sprouts
dinner	Curried carrots

Keep a Chart (Week 1)

DAY OF THE WEEK (six hour intervals)		SIZE/LENGTH (measured In mm.)	CHANGE (measured In mm.)	REASON FOR CHANGE (magazine read, movie seen)
MONDAY	9am			
	3pm			
	9pm			
	3am			
TUESDAY	9am			
	3pm			
	9pm			
	3am			
WEDNESDAY	9am			
	3pm			
	9pm			
	3am			
THURSDAY	9am			
	3pm			
	9pm			
	3am			
FRIDAY	9am			
	3pm			
	9pm			
	3am			
SATURDAY	9am			
	3pm			
	9pm			
	3am			
SUNDAY	9am			
	3pm			
	9pm			
	3am			

Keep a Chart (Week 2)

DAY OF THE WEEK (six hour intervals)		SIZE/LENGTH (measured In mm.)	CHANGE (measured In mm.)	REASON FOR CHANGE (magazine read, movie seen)
MONDAY	9am			
	3pm			
	9pm			
	3am			
TUESDAY	9am			
	3pm			
	9pm			
	3am			
WEDNESDAY	9am			
	3pm			
	9pm			
	3am			
THURSDAY	9am			
	3pm			
	9pm			
	3am			
FRIDAY	9am			
	3pm			
	9pm			
	3am			
SATURDAY	9am			
	3pm			
	9pm			
	3am			
SUNDAY	9am			
	3pm			
	9pm			
	3am			

If All Fails To Convince Them

If all fails to convince them that you're not small, then just tell them straight.

"IT'S THERE

I TELL YOU

... ARE YOU

BLIND?"

It's There I Tell You ...

A Friend in Need

Please send a copy of this book 'Size Isn't Everything' to someone I know who could really benefit from it. Please include the message below. I have enclosed a cheque/postal order for £1.99 made payable to IDEAS UNLIMITED (PUBLISHING)

Send To: ....

Message: ....

Address: ....

....

....

County: .... Post Code: ....

Please send your completed coupon with your payment to:

IDEAS UNLIMITED (PUBLISHING)
PO BOX 125
PORTSMOUTH
HAMPSHIRE PO1 4PP

Other Titles available from Ideas Unlimited (Publishing)

Please send me (Postage free UK):

copies "100 CHAT UP LINES"
ISBN: 1 871964 00 8 (128 pages A7) @ £1.99

copies "THE IDIOTS HANDBOOK OF LOVE & SEX"
ISBN: 1 871964 08 3 (128 pages A7) @ £1.99

copies "10 GOLDEN RULES OF CHATTING UP"
ISBN: 1 871964 09 1 (128 pages A7) @ £1.99

copies "SIZE ISN'T EVERYTHING"
ISBN: 1 871964 12 1 (64 pages A7) @ £1.99

copies "OF COURSE I LOVE YOU"
ISBN: 1 871964 01 6 (96 pages A6) @ £1.99

copies "WELL HUNG"
ISBN: 1 871964 07 5 (96 pages A5) @ £2.99

copies "BODY LANGUAGE SEX SIGNALS"
ISBN: 1 871964 06 7 (64 pages) @ £2.50

copies "BEGINNERS GUIDE TO KISSING"
ISBN: 1 871964 02 4 (64 pages A5) @ £2.50

copies "TIPS FOR A SUCCESSFUL MARRIAGE"
ISBN: 1 871964 03 2 (64 pages A5) @ £2.50

copies "JOY OF FATHERHOOD"
ISBN: 1 871964 04 0 (64 pages A5) @ £2.50

copies "OFFICE HANKY PANKY"
ISBN: 1 871964 05 9 (64 pages A5) @ £2.50

copies "SPORT FOR THE ELDERLY"
ISBN: 1 871964 11 3 (48 pages A5) @ £2.50

copies "HAVE YOU SEEN THE NOTICE BOARD?"
ISBN: 1 871964 10 5 (80 pages A4) @ £3.99

P.T.O.

I have enclosed a cheque/postal order for £............................
made payable to IDEAS UNLIMITED (PUBLISHING)

NAME: ....

ADDRESS: ....

....

....

....

COUNTY: .... POST CODE: ....

Fill in the coupon above and send it with your payment to:

IDEAS UNLIMITED (PUBLISHING)
PO BOX 125
PORTSMOUTH
HAMPSHIRE
PO1 4PP

Postage free within the UK.

If you wish your purchase to be sent directly to someone else (eg, Birthday, Christmas, Wedding, Valentines Gift), simply fill in their name and address in the coupon above and enclose your cheque/postal order with your personal message or card, if desired. We will be pleased to send your gift directly to your chosen recipient.

Other Titles available from
Ideas Unlimited (Publishing)

Please send me (Postage free UK):

copies "100 CHAT UP LINES"
ISBN: 1 871964 00 8 (128 pages A7) @ £1.99

copies "THE IDIOTS HANDBOOK OF LOVE & SEX"
ISBN: 1 871964 08 3 (128 pages A7) @ £1.99

copies "10 GOLDEN RULES OF CHATTING UP"
ISBN: 1 871964 09 1 (128 pages A7) @ £1.99

copies "SIZE ISN'T EVERYTHING"
ISBN: 1 871964 12 1 (64 pages A7) @ £1.99

copies "OF COURSE I LOVE YOU"
ISBN: 1 871964 01 6 (96 pages A6) @ £1.99

copies "WELL HUNG"
ISBN: 1 871964 07 5 (96 pages A5) @ £2.99

copies "BODY LANGUAGE SEX SIGNALS"
ISBN: 1 871964 06 7 (64 pages) @ £2.50

copies "BEGINNERS GUIDE TO KISSING"
ISBN: 1 871964 02 4 (64 pages A5) @ £2.50

copies "TIPS FOR A SUCCESSFUL MARRIAGE"
ISBN: 1 871964 03 2 (64 pages A5) @ £2.50

copies "JOY OF FATHERHOOD"
ISBN: 1 871964 04 0 (64 pages A5) @ £2.50

copies "OFFICE HANKY PANKY"
ISBN: 1 871964 05 9 (64 pages A5) @ £2.50

copies "SPORT FOR THE ELDERLY"
ISBN: 1 871964 11 3 (48 pages A5) @ £2.50

copies "HAVE YOU SEEN THE NOTICE BOARD?"
ISBN: 1 871964 10 5 (80 pages A4) @ £3.99

P.T.O.

I have enclosed a cheque/postal order for £...........................
made payable to IDEAS UNLIMITED (PUBLISHING)

NAME: ....

ADDRESS: ....

....

....

....

COUNTY: .... POST CODE: ....

Fill in the coupon above and send it with your payment to:

IDEAS UNLIMITED (PUBLISHING)
PO BOX 125
PORTSMOUTH
HAMPSHIRE
PO1 4PP

Postage free within the UK.

If you wish your purchase to be sent directly to someone else (eg, Birthday, Christmas, Wedding, Valentines Gift), simply fill in their name and address in the coupon above and enclose your cheque/postal order with your personal message or card, if desired. We will be pleased to send your gift directly to your chosen recipient.

How To Use Your Free Gift

We have enclosed a free gift with this book, which we feel will be an invaluable tool in keeping track of your situation as well as helping you acquire that most important self-confidence. Who said how big an inch should be, and what gives them the right to set these important facts. As far as you are concerned the ruler enclosed is a twelve inch ruler, and you know that the manufacturers can't be wrong.

USERS INSTRUCTIONS

1. Choose a very bright area, preferably outside in the open air.

2. Pull your shorts down to your knees.

3. Hold the ruler with your right hand, leaving your left hand free for the search.

4. Make sure that your willy is in the full upright position.

5. Hold the ruler next to your willy, or where you think your willy should be.

6. Read the measurements to the nearest twelve inches.

7. Record the measurements on the chart provided and keep a close eye on your progress.

Use Your Free Gift With Confidence

THE RULER ENCLOSED WITH THIS BOOK IS A LARGER MODEL OF THE ORIGINAL DESIGN. SHOULD YOU REQUIRE A SMALL MODEL, PLEASE BREAK THE RULER IN HALF AND REWRITE THE NUMBERS.